DON'T THROW IT AWAY...CRAFT IT!

Cool Crafts with
Plastic

Jane Yates

WINDMILL
BOOKS

Published in 2018 by **Windmill Books**,
an Imprint of Rosen Publishing
29 East 21st Street, New York, NY 10010

Developed and produced for Rosen by BlueApple*Works* Inc.

Creative Director: Melissa McClellan
Managing Editor for BlueApple*Works*: Melissa McClellan
Designer: T.J. Choleva
Photo Research: Jane Reid
Editor: Janice Dyer
Craft Artisans: Janet Kompare-Fritz (p. 8, 20); Jane Yates (p. 18, 26); Jerrie McClellan (p. 10, 12, 14, 16, 22, 24, 28)

Photo Credits: cover upper right Serdar Tibet/Shutterstock.com; cover, back cover middle pryzmat/Shutterstock.
com; background paper cover, TOC Becky Starsmore/Shutterstock.com; cover center Coltty/Shutterstock.com;
page backgrounds Pavel Kubarkov/Shutterstock.com; p. 4 top Ermolaevamariya/Dreamstime.com; p. 4 middle
Elena Elisseeva/Shutterstock.com; p. 4 bottom Alaettin YILDIRIM/Shutterstock.com; p. 5 top to bottom and left to
right: Photka/Dreamstime.com; kontur-vid/Shutterstock.com; Sappachoats/Shutterstock.com; Freedom_Studio/
Shutterstock.com; Garsya/Shutterstock.com; Gradts/Dreamstime.com; monticello/Shutterstock.com; Samantha
Roberts/Shutterstock.com; GeniusKp/Shutterstock.com; Nataliia K/Shutterstock.com; photosync/Shutterstock.com;
Lyudmila Suvorova/Shutterstock.com; Sergey Mostovoy/Dreamstime.com; p. 6 top crabgarden/Shutterstock.com; p. 7
bottom right KDS444/Creative Commons; p. 9 Arlene Gapusan/Shutterstock.com; p. 10 right Rich Carey/Shutterstock.
com; p. 11 design56/Shutterstock.com; p. 12 right Albert Karimov/Shutterstock.com; p. 14 right wavebreakmedia/
Shutterstock.com; p. 18 right Jose Angel Astor Rocha/Shutterstock.com; p. 20 Coltty/Shutterstock.com; p. 21 Mark
Rooks/Shutterstock.com; p. 22 right Gmgadani/Shutterstock.com; p. 24 Jan H Andersen/Shutterstock.com; p. 26
right K. Roy Zerloch/Shutterstock.com; p. 28 De Jongh Photography/Shutterstock.com; p. 29 bottom Lee Yiu Tung/
Shutterstock.com; All craft photography Austen Photography

Cataloging-in-Publication Data

Names: Yates, Jane.
Title: Cool crafts with plastic / Jane Yates.
Description: New York : Windmill Books, 2018. | Series: Don't throw it away...craft it! | Includes index.
Identifiers: ISBN 9781499482904 (pbk.) | ISBN 9781499482843 (library bound) | ISBN 9781499482652 (6 pack)
Subjects: LCSH: Plastics craft--Juvenile literature. | Plastics--Recycling--Juvenile literature. | Salvage (Waste, etc.)--
Juvenile literature. | Handicraft--Juvenile literature.
Classification: LCC TT297.Y38 2018 | DDC 745.57'2--dc23

Manufactured in the United States of America
CPSIA Compliance Information: Batch #BS17WM For Further Information contact: Rosen Publishing, New York, New York at 1-800-237-9932

CONTENTS

GETTING STARTED

To make great paper crafts, you need the right materials and a **makerspace** where you can think and create. Your family may have a permanent makerspace set up for crafting, or you can create one whenever you need it. You also may already have many of the supplies shown here. Your family can buy anything else you need at a craft store or dollar store. Organize your supplies in boxes or plastic bins, and you will be ready to create in your makerspace.

A note about patterns

Some of the crafts in this book use patterns or **templates**. Trace the pattern, cut the pattern, and then place it on the material you want to cut out. You can either tape it in place and cut both the pattern and material, or trace around the pattern onto the material and then cut it out.

RECYCLABLES

You can make all of the crafts in this book with materials found around the house. Save recyclables (newspapers, used wrapping paper, tissue paper, magazines, flyers, junk mail and more) to use in your craft projects. You can even use the back of old greeting cards when you need card stock for your craft. Use your imagination and have fun!

A note about measurements

Measurements are given in U.S. form with metric in parentheses. The metric conversion is rounded to the nearest whole number to make it easier to measure.

PAINT

RULER

SCISSORS

PLASTIC LIDS

GLUE AND TAPE

PAINTBRUSHES

BOTTLE TOPS

SEQUINS & STICK-ON GEMS

BAMBOO SKEWERS

RIBBON & YARN

GLITTER

PENCIL

TISSUE PAPER

FELT

PIPE CLEANERS

TECHNIQUES

Have fun while making your plastic crafts, and be creative. Your projects do not have to look just like the ones in this book. Instead, you can mix and match many of the ideas in the book to come up with your own **unique** projects. Use the following techniques to create your plastic crafts.

PREPARING PLASTIC CONTAINERS FOR CRAFTS

- Make sure to clean your containers so there are no bits of food or liquid left in them.

- Remove the label. Some come off easily. If the label is hard to remove, soak the jar in warm soapy water for 20 minutes. It should come off easily after that.

PAPER-MACHE GLUE

- Add equal amounts of white glue and water in a bowl. Mix the glue and water together with a spoon. If you have leftover glue, put it in a container with a lid and use it later. (An empty yogurt container works well.)

Tip

When working with tissue paper and paper-mache glue, be very gentle. Tissue paper rips very easily. Don't try to smooth it out, the creases can be part of the look. If adding more glue, dab the glue with an up-and-down motion rather than trying to brush glue over the tissue paper.

Tip

Paper-mache is messy! Cover your work station with newspaper or a garbage bag.

An adult should supervise whenever a project in this book requires using sharp instruments. Even then, everyone needs to be careful when using sharp instruments.

PAPER-MACHE TECHNIQUE

- Prepare your base. You can make bases out of plastic bottles or balloons.
- Tear squares of tissue paper.
- Mix together your paper-mache glue.
- Use a paintbrush to coat the surface of the base. Place the squares one at a time on the base. Overlap the direction of the strips to create an even surface. Completely cover the base.
- Set the base aside to dry. This usually takes a full day.

PAPER-MACHE SHAPES

- To make paper-mache shapes, coat the surface of several strips with glue and then press together to make a wad.
- Squeeze out the extra glue, then form the wad into the desired shape.
- Add it to the base and let it dry completely.

WEAVING

- When strips of paper or cloth are interlaced in a pattern, the process is called weaving. The **horizontal** strips go across over and under the **perpendicular** strips. The finished weaving is much stronger than the individual strips.

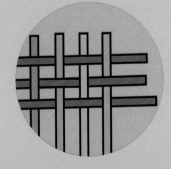

BE PREPARED

- Read through the instructions and make sure you have all the materials you need.
- Clean up when you are finished making your crafts. Put away your supplies for next time.

BE SAFE

- Ask for help when you need it.
- Ask for permission to borrow tools.
- Be careful when using scissors and needles.

YOU'LL NEED:

- Milk jug
- Tissue paper
- Scissors
- Pencil
- Glue
- Black marker
- Googly eyes

DID YOU KNOW?

We are making more plastic today than ever before. In fact, worldwide, more plastic was produced in the last 10 years than in the entire 20th century! Half of this plastic is used once and then thrown away.

1 Mark

2 Cut

3 Cover with tissue paper

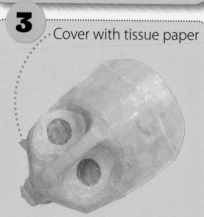

Milk jug Mask

Make a decorative mask out of a milk jug to hang on the wall! Make one like this or use the techniques to create a different mask.

1 Make a line around the jug from top to bottom with a black marker. The handle should be in the middle of one of the halves you created.

2 Have an adult cut the milk jug in half by following the line. Have them make sure there are no sharp edges. You will use the piece with the handle for your mask. Recycle or save the other half for another craft!

3 Mix a container of paper-mache glue. Cut squares of tissue paper. Apply the tissue paper to the jug. Cut different colors of tissue paper in smaller pieces to make the eyes.

4 Cut 2-inch (5 cm) by 2-inch (5 cm) squares of tissue paper in different colors. Twist one square around the end of a pencil. Dip it in glue and stick it to the top of the mask to make hair.

5 Repeat twisting tissue paper squares and gluing them until the entire top of the mask is covered.

6 Using the shaping technique described on page 7, make a nose, eyebrows, and mouth with tissue paper and paper-mache glue.

7 Glue the facial features to the mask. Glue googly eyes to the mask.

You can also make the mask for wearing instead of decoration. Cut two holes for eyes and one for the mouth. Staple a piece of elastic to either side of the mask.

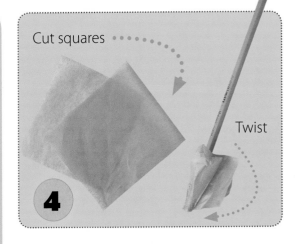

4 Cut squares ... Twist

5 Glue

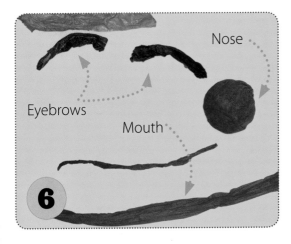

6 Eyebrows ... Nose ... Mouth

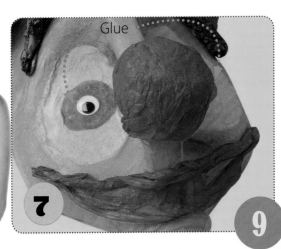

7 Glue

9

YOU'LL NEED:

- Clear plastic lids
- Pencil and paper
- Tape
- Glue (that dries clear)
- Glitter
- Tiny beads
- Stick-on gems
- Permament markers
- Thread and needle

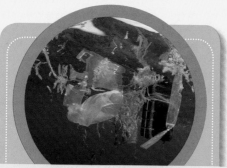

DID YOU KNOW?

The Great Pacific Garbage Patch is located off the coast of California. It spans the ocean between North America and Japan. This large ocean garbage site is made up mostly of plastic. A lot of it is made up of microplastics which are tiny pieces of plastic. Some microplastics are so small you can't even see them, but they are still harmful to the environment.

Suncatcher

You can hang suncatchers in your window and watch them sparkle in the sunlight.

1 Place a clear plastic lid on a piece of a paper. Trace around it. Sketch your design on the paper inside the circle. You can use the patterns on page 30 or make your own. Place the lid back on top of the design. Tape it in place.

2 On the lid, cover part of the design with glue. Do one color at a time, until you have filled in the whole design. Sprinkle glitter or small beads on top. You can also use stick-on gems. Remove the tape. Let it dry.

3 Tap the lid lightly over a piece of a paper to get rid of beads or glitter that did not stick. Color the edge of the lid with permanent markers.

4 Thread a needle and thread. To make a hanger, push the needle through the top of the lid. Pull some of the thread through. Remove the needle and tie the two pieces together, making a knot.

> You could also draw your design with glitter glue. It is easier and less messy to work with, but takes longer to dry.

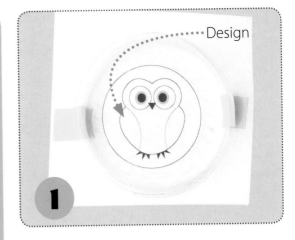

1 ·········· Design

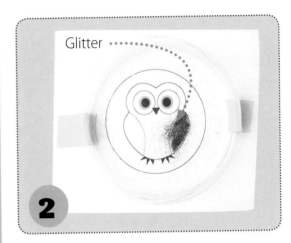

Glitter ··········

2

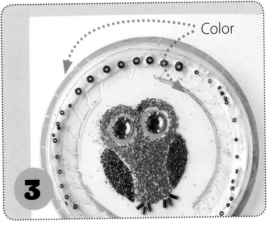

Color ·········

3

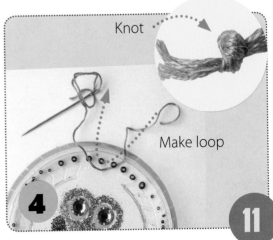

Knot ·········

Make loop

4

YOU'LL NEED:

- Bottle tops (small)
- Lid (from liquid detergent)
- Card stock
- Felt scraps
- Bamboo skewers
- Marker or paint
- Tape
- Pipe cleaners
- Scissors
- Modeling clay
- Colored tape
- Glue (that dries clear)

DID YOU KNOW?

Americans use 2.5 million plastic bottles every hour and throw away 35 billion plastic bottles every year. Most of the cost of a bottle of water is for packaging, shipping, and **marketing**, not for the water itself.

Flowerpot

Make a beautiful pot of flowers out of bottle tops and plastic lids from laundry detergent.

1 Cover a square of card stock with glue. Arrange the lids on top of it in the shape of a flower. Leave it to dry. Trim the card stock around the bottle tops when dry.

2 Make a stem from a bamboo skewer. Color it green with a marker or paint. Tape it to the back of the flower.

3 Wrap a pipe cleaner around the stick and make two loops for leaves.

4 Fill the lid three quarters full with modeling clay. Decorate the lid with colored tape.

5 Stick the stem into the modeling clay.

Another way to make flowers is to glue a piece of card stock to the back of a large lid (such as from a mayonnaise jar.) Trim when dry. Glue the bottle tops directly to the front of the large lid. Another way to make the stem is to glue or tape two popsicle sticks together. Cover the sticks with felt. Cut out felt leaves and glue to the sticks. Go on to step 4.

1 Leave room for the stem

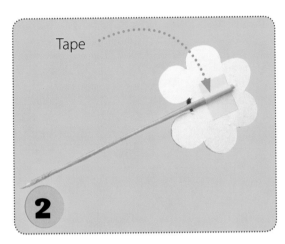

Tape

2

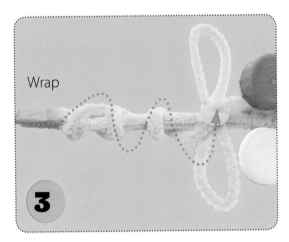

Wrap

3

Fill with modeling clay

4 Tape

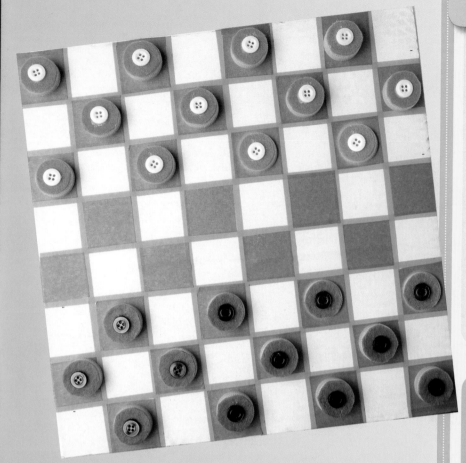

YOU'LL NEED:

- 24 bottle tops
- 24 buttons
- Felt (2 colors)
- Scissors
- Glue
- Cardboard
- White paint and brush
- Ruler
- Narrow masking tape and painter's tape

DID YOU KNOW?

Checkers is a strategy board game for two players. The goal is to remove all your opponent's pieces from the board. Players take turns moving **diagonally** on the board to an empty square, or they can jump over their opponent's piece to capture it. You win the game if you remove all your opponent's pieces, or if your opponent can't make a move.

Checkers

Make your own checkerboard and set of markers and challenge a friend to a game.

1 Cut one piece of felt into 12 squares slightly larger than the bottle tops. Do the same with the other color.

2 Cover the surface of a bottle top with glue and place on one of the squares. Repeat for all the bottle tops.

3 Trim around the bottle tops. Glue a button to the top for decoration.

4 Cut a piece of cardboard that is 12 inches by 12 inches (30 cm × 30 cm) in size. Paint both sides white. Starting at one corner, make marks with a pencil 1½ inches (4 cm) apart all around the board.

5 Using narrow tape, pull the tape from one mark to the opposite mark, or use a marker and ruler and draw lines. Continue doing this until you have a checkerboard pattern.

6 Starting at one end of the board, use paint or cut squares of painter's tape to fill in alternating squares on the board.

You can make a travel board using self-adhesive shelf liner with a checkerboard pattern. Cut a piece slightly larger than 8 squares by 8 squares. Fold each edge over and cover the sticky part with a piece of felt

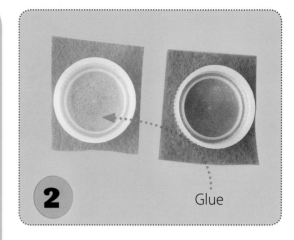

2 Glue

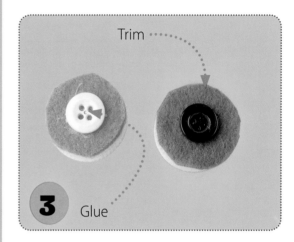

Trim

3 Glue

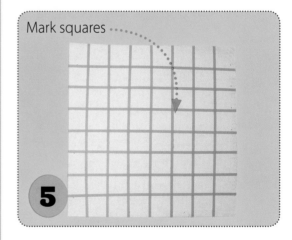

Mark squares

5

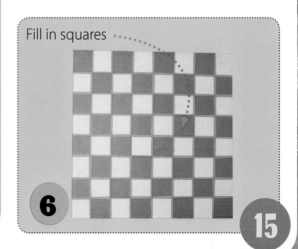

Fill in squares

6

YOU'LL NEED:

- **Cardboard**
- **String**
- **Tape**
- **Plastic bags**
  (different colors)
- **Scissors**

2

Tape

3

Fold

Cut   Cut

4

Cut Strips

Placemat

Keep plastic bags out of the garbage by making this cool placemat.

1 Cut a rectangle out of cardboard. A good size is 9 inches by 12 inches (23 cm × 30 cm). But you can make it bigger or smaller.

2 Tape the end of the string to one side of the cardboard in the middle. Wind the string around the board about ½ inch (1 cm) apart. When you get to the other side, cut the string and tape it in place. Secure the string in place with a piece of tape across the back of the cardboard.

3 Fold the bags so the handles are together and straighten them out. Fold over twice. Cut off the handles and the bottoms of the bags.

4 Cut strips about 2 inches (5 cm) wide.

5 Keeping the strip flat, weave through the string, over then under. Leave about 3 inches (8 cm) on each end. Weave the second one using alternate strings.

6 Gently press the first string down with your fingers to look like rope. Do the same with the second.

7 Tie the two ends on each side together in a double knot, but not so tight that you pull the strips out.

8 Continue weaving, repeating steps 5, 6, and 7 until the mat is the size you'd like.

9 Cutting two at a time, cut strings in the middle on one side of the tape. Tie those at the edges of the mat. Trim excess string. Do the same for the other side of the matt. Continue until all strings are tied.

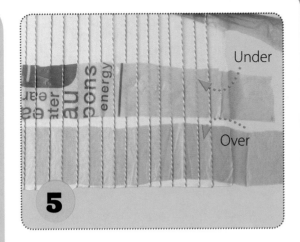

5 Under / Over

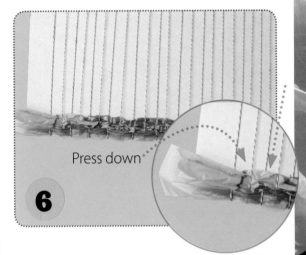

6 Press down

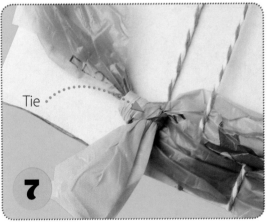

7 Tie

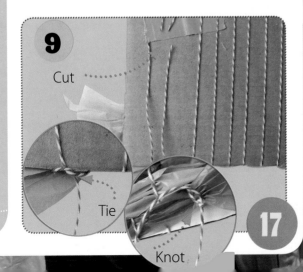

9 Cut / Tie / Knot

YOU'LL NEED:

- Plastic container
- Craft foam
- Felt
- Cardboard
- Scissors
- String
- Tape
- Googly eyes

DID YOU KNOW?

Experts have estimated that it takes 450 to 1,000 years for plastic to break down. As a result, every piece of plastic that has ever been made still exists in some shape or form, except for the small amount that has been burned.

Ball and Cup Game

In a ball and cup style game, the idea is to toss the ball and catch it in the cup. In this case, the puppy catches the bone.

1 Using the patterns on pages 30–31, make templates to cut out the ears, tongue, and tail from craft foam and felt.

2 Using the patterns on page 31, make templates to cut out legs, eyes, and nose from craft foam and felt. Glue the googly eyes on the eyes you cut out. Draw lines on the bottom of the legs to make paws.

3 Glue the tail, ears, tongue, nose, eyes, and legs to your container.

4 Using the pattern on page 30, cut out two bone shapes from cardboard. Cut a piece of string. Glue the string on one of the bones and glue the two bones together, so the string is in the middle. Tape the other end of the string to the inside of the container.

If you prefer cats, you can make the container into a cat. Make short pointed ears instead of floppy ones. Instead of a bone, you could make it a ball of yarn. Roll a small ball of yarn. Tie another piece around it securely and then attach that to the container.

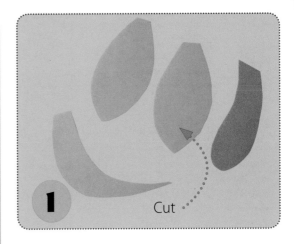

1 Cut

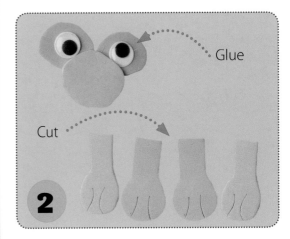

Glue

Cut

2

Glue

3

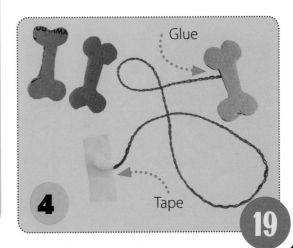

Glue

4 Tape

YOU'LL NEED:

- Plastic bottle
- Cardboard
- Scissors
- Paint and markers
- Glue
- Pine or spruce cones

Tip

Make several hedgehogs using pine cones, spruce cones, and other nature materials. Place them around your garden as great year-round decorations.

Bottle Hedgehog

Make this cute hedgehog from a plastic bottle and pine or spruce cones.

1. Paint the bottle and cap. Brown paint works well for the bottle and black or darker brown works well for the cap. Leave to dry.

2. Using the pattern on page 31, make templates of the eyes and trace their shapes on a piece of cardboard. Paint and cut them out once they are dry.

3. Using the pattern on page 31, make templates of the ears and trace their shapes on cardboard. Paint and cut them out once they are dry. Bend the bottom of the ears over to make a tab. Put glue on the tab and glue to the bottle.

4. Glue the cones to the bottle. If using spruce cones, lay some sideways to support the others. You can also break some in half to make them shorter.

5. Glue the eyes to the bottle. Draw a mouth and eyebrows with a black marker.

You can use regular glue for this project. Use blobs of it rather than a little drop. If you can use a low-temperature glue gun with an adult's help, that would work very well for this project as well.

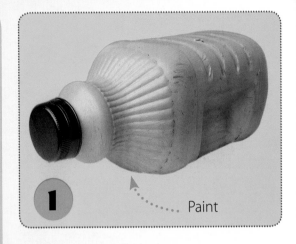

1 Paint

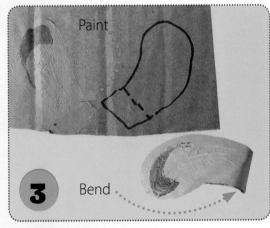

2 Paint

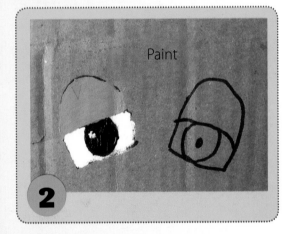

3 Paint

Bend

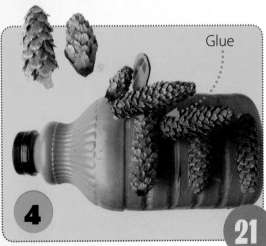

4 Glue

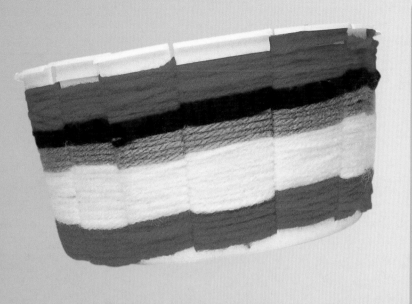

YOU'LL NEED:

- Plastic tub container
- Scissors
- Yarn scraps
- Glue (that dries clear) or tape
- Felt

DID YOU KNOW?

Every year we throw away enough plastic to circle Earth four times. It is important to reduce, reuse, and recycle plastic to save the environment and protect wildlife.

Woven Bowl

Make a cool woven bowl from a plastic tub and some leftover yarn.

1 Cut from the top of the tub to the bottom. Repeat these cuts at about 1-inch (3 cm) intervals. Make sure you end up with an odd number of strips.

2 If you are using thick yarn, one strand will work, but if your yarn is thin, use two strands at once. Start at the bottom of the tub on the inside. Leaving about 2 inches (5 cm) of extra yarn, start weaving the yarn in and out of the plastic strips, around the tub. When you finish the first row, reverse the direction. Continue weaving the rest of the bowl in this direction.

3 When you want to change color, leave another 2 inches (5 cm) on the inside and cut the yarn. Start with a new color leaving 2 inches (5 cm) and then start weaving where you left off with the first color.

4 Continue to weave, changing colors to make stripes until you get to the top of the tub. Push the wool down every few rows.

5 Glue or tape all the inside ends to the inside of the bowl. Optional: Glue yarn around the top to cover the plastic edges as shown in left middle image. Cut a circle of felt and glue it to the bottom inside.

Try making the bowl with plastic bag strips. Prepare the strips as shown on pages 16–17. Tie the strips together. Try painting the tub before you weave. Follow the same steps as described above for yarn.

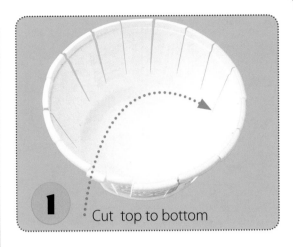

1 Cut top to bottom

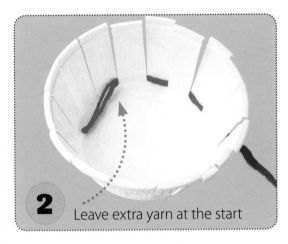

2 Leave extra yarn at the start

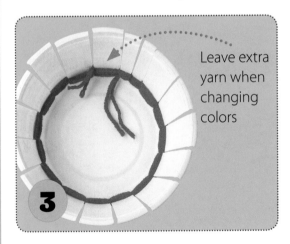

Leave extra yarn when changing colors

3

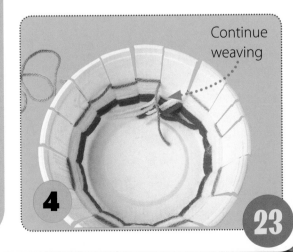

Continue weaving

4

YOU'LL NEED:

- Bottle tops
- Felt scaps
- Clue
- Scissors
- Googly eyes, beads, and string
- Markers
- Card stock
- Magnets

DID YOU KNOW?

Magnets are materials that create a magnetic field. You can't see the magnetic field, but it pulls the magnet to certain types of metals, such as iron, nickel, and cobalt. Magnets are not attracted to wood, plastic, glass, fabric, silver, gold, and other metals.

Bottle Top Magnets

Turn bottle caps and felt into fun magnets.

1. Cover the top of the bottle top with glue and lay it upside down on a square of felt. Turn it over and trim around the bottle top.

2. Decorate by gluing on googly eyes, beads, pieces of felt, or string. You can make marks like those on the strawberry using a permanent marker.

3. Put glue along the edges of the bottom of the tops. Place onto a piece of card stock and leave to dry. Trim around the top.

4. Attach magnets to the card stock on the back of the bottle top. Some have adhesive backing, but if the one you have doesn't, you can use glue. When removing the magnets from a metal surface, slide them rather than pulling them or the magnet may come off.

You can also make big magnets using the lids from jars. Follow the same steps as above. You may have to use more than one magnet on the back.

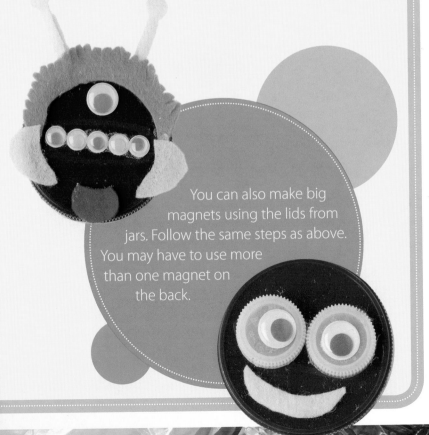

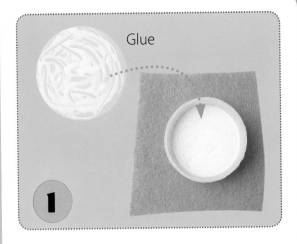

Glue

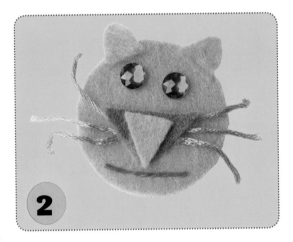

Glue

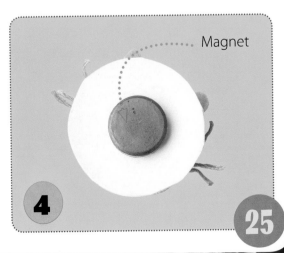

Magnet

- Plastic lid (thin and bendable)
- Cardboard
- Glue
- Decorative stones
- String
- Scissors

DID YOU KNOW?

A mosaic is a piece of art made using small pieces of stone, colored glass, or other materials. Mosaics are an ancient type of artwork. Some have been found from around 3000 BC. The first mosaics were made of stones, shells, and pieces of ivory.

Mosaic Decoration

Mosaic decorations make great gifts or you can use them to decorate your room.

1 Start with a clean plastic lid. It must be thin and bendable so you can get the decoration out of the lid when it is dry. Set it on a piece of cardboard.

2 Arrange the stones in the plastic lid. The part of the stone you would like to be face out in the final decoration must go facedown in the lid.

3 Cut a small piece of string. Fold it in half and make a knot at the end.

4 Place the string on top of the stones at one end of the lid.

5 Fill the lid with glue, and make sure all the stones and knotted part of the string are covered. (Remove the lid of the glue to pour. Pour very carefully. You don't want the lid to overflow.)

6 Place your decoration on the piece of cardboard somewhere out of the way to dry. It may take anywhere from several days to a week to dry. Peel the lid away from the decoration. If the glue is still wet, leave it until the glue is dry, then peel away the lid.

You can also decorate your mosaic with glitter and shiny sequins. Follow the same steps as above, but add more glitter and sequins after you have poured the glue.

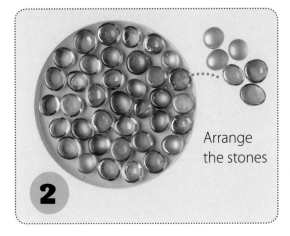

2 Arrange the stones

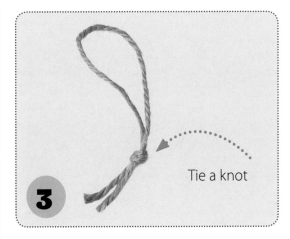

3 Tie a knot

Place the string

4

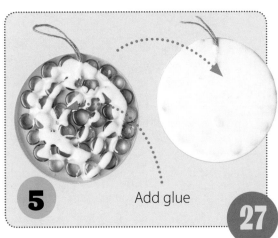

5 Add glue

- **Bottle tops**
- **Background material (old photo frame, cardboard)**
- **Glue (that dries clear)**
- **Glitter**
- **Paint**
- **Stick-on gems**
- **Ribbon**
- **Decorative tape**
- **String**

DID YOU KNOW?

Plastic bottle caps are one of the most common items found during beach cleanups. The caps are made from a different type of plastic than plastic bottles. Recycled bottle caps can be used to make toothbrushes, razors, plates, cutlery, measuring cups, and cutting boards.

Bottle Top Art

You can make beautiful art from bottle tops. Learn how to make flowers or come up with your own creation using the examples as inspiration.

1 Paint the background. Add some glitter to the paint. Draw a design.

2 Many bottle tops are white. To make some more interesting colors for your picture, paint some or coat the top in glue and dip in glitter. Add some stick-on gems to decorate them.

3 Cut pieces of ribbon or decorative tape for stems and leaves. Glue or stick them to the background.

4 Arrange the tops on the background in a flower design. Fill a wide lid with glue. Remove a top from the board, dip it in glue, and replace it on the board. Repeat until you have glued all of the tops.

5 Make a border with decorative tape. Put one piece along each edge. Punch two holes in the top of your picture. Thread a piece of string through both holes and make a knot.

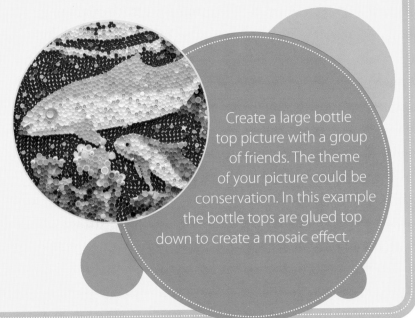

Create a large bottle top picture with a group of friends. The theme of your picture could be conservation. In this example the bottle tops are glued top down to create a mosaic effect.

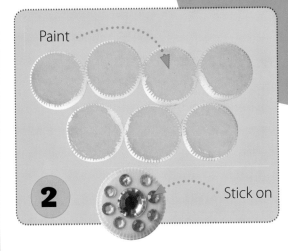

Paint

Stick on

2

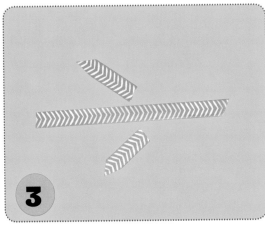

3

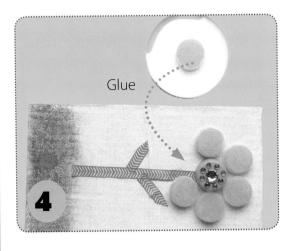

Glue

4

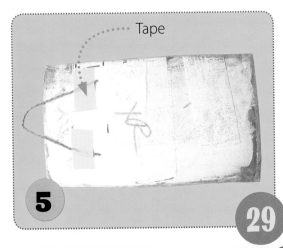

Tape

5

PATTERNS

Patterns for sun catchers on page 10

Tail

Bone

cut 2

Tongue

Patterns for ball and cup game
on page 18

Patterns for the bottle hedgehog on page 20

Ears

Eyes

Patterns for ball and cup game on page 18

Legs

cut 4

Ears

Eyes

Nose

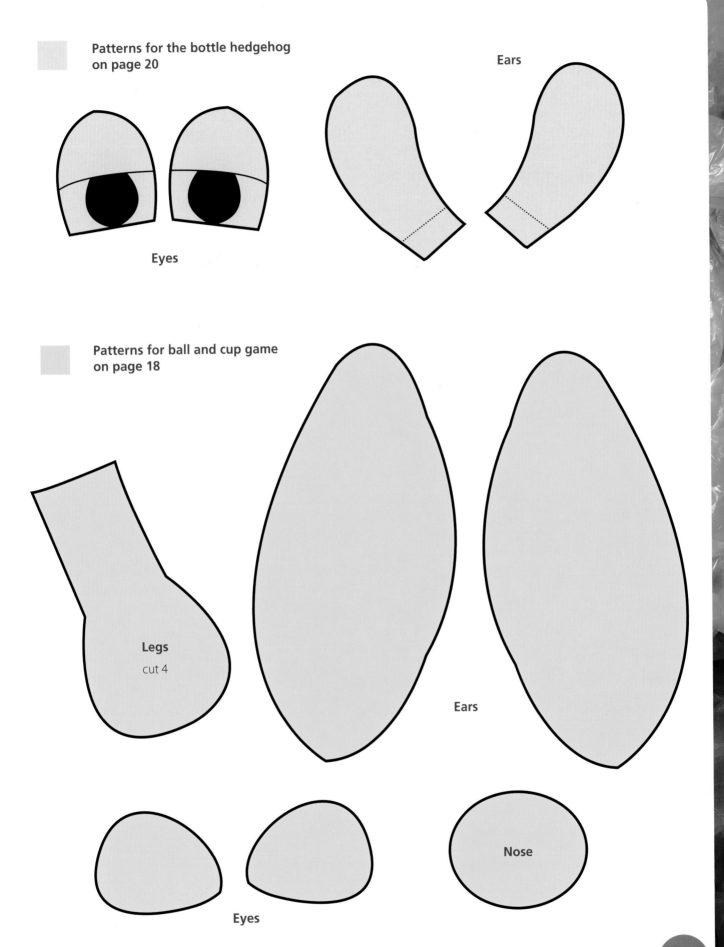

GLOSSARY

diagonally Having a slanted direction.

horizontal Going from side to side, in the same direction as the horizon.

makerspace A place to create, invent, explore, and discover.

marketing Ways of promoting and selling products.

perpendicular Vertical; straight up and down.

template A pattern to use as a guide.

unique One of a kind.

FOR MORE INFORMATION

FURTHER READING

Elliot, Marion. *Recycled Craft Projects for Kids.* Helotes, TX: Armadillo, 2014.

Jones, Jen. *Cool Crafts with Newspapers, Magazines, and Junk Mail.* North Mankato, MN: Capstone Press, 2011.

WEBSITES

For web resources related to the subject of this book, go to: **www.windmillbooks.com/weblinks** and select this book's title.

INDEX